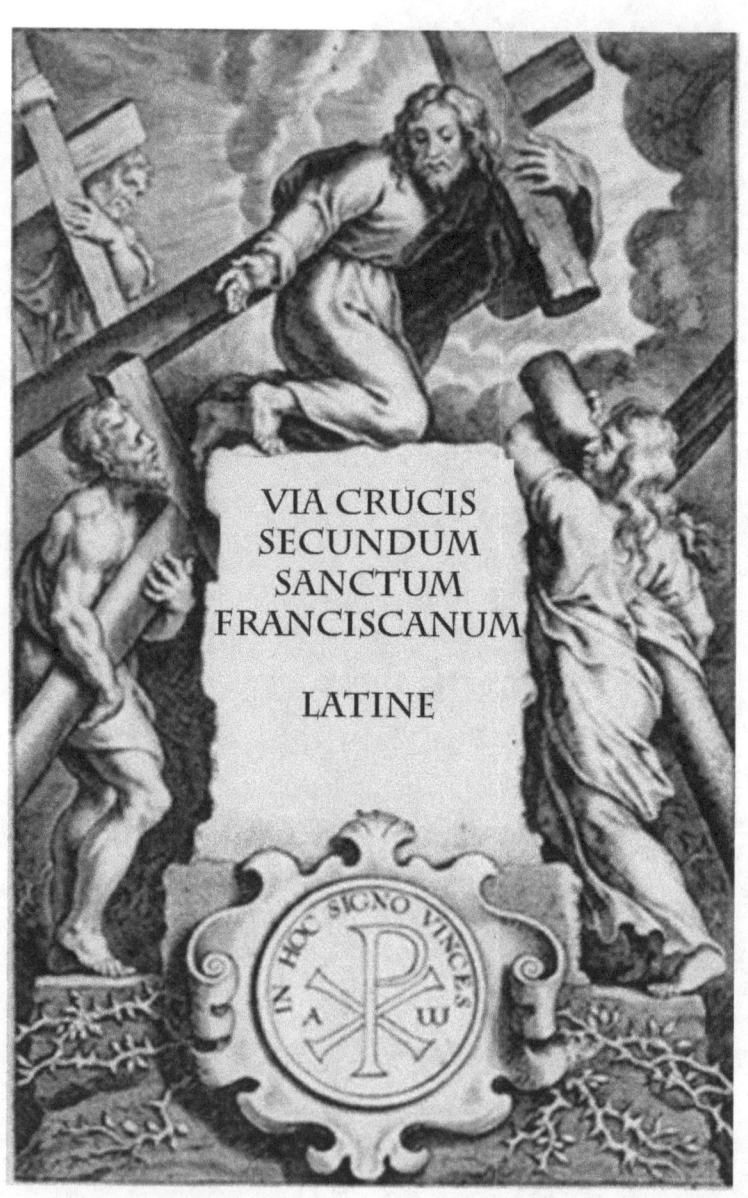

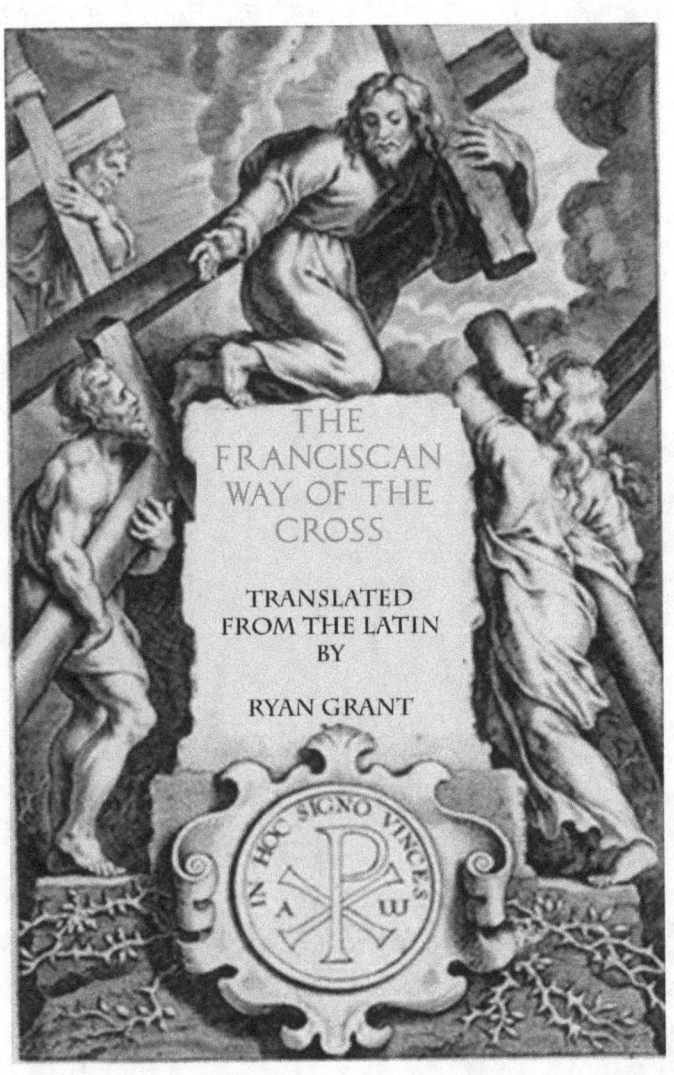

THE FRANCISCAN WAY OF THE CROSS

TRANSLATED FROM THE LATIN BY

RYAN GRANT

Exercitium Sanctæ Crucis

The Franciscan Way of the Cross

Latin - English

Translated and Edited from the Latin
by Ryan Grant

MEDIATRIX PRESS

MMXIV

© Mediatrix Press, 2014. All Rights reserved. No part of this work may be reproduced in electronic or physical format, except for reviews or classroom use, without the explicit permission of the publisher.

Mediatrix Press
607 E. 6th Ave.
Post Falls, ID 83854
www.mediatrixpress.com

Preface

I have endeavored to provide here, a way for Catholics to experience the way of the Cross in the Church's language, Latin, as well as to carry it out in English. Some who only know a little Latin might prefer to say the familiar prayers in Latin, while carrying out the Meditations in English; whereas those who are more advanced might wish to make the meditations in Latin. Some might prefer to do it all in English. Thus, this book may be used by those at all levels of Latin.

In making the translations, I have stayed dutifully faithful to traditional renderings in English for common prayers, while for the meditations and closing prayers I have striven to make a more literal rendering.

I have also added the Seraphic Rosary, which also known as the Franciscan Crown, provided with the prayers said by Franciscan Tertiaries when praying it.

I hope, that these prayers will help all who pray them attain a deeper love of Christ, who is the source and summit of the whole Christian life.

Ryan Grant
Mediatrix Press

Art Credits

All artwork is in the public domain.

Cover art: *St. Francis meditating on death*
-Michaelangelo Merisi da Caravaggio

Right: *Stigmata of St. Francis*
-Tiziano

Woodcuts of the Stations
-Guardian Angel Prayerbook
Belgium, 1884

Cum Beatus Franciscus oraret in latere Montis Alvernae, vidit Christum in specie seraphim crucifixi, qui impressit in manibus et pedibus et etiam in latere dextro Stigmata Crucis ejusdem Domini nostri Jesu Christi.
-*Legendo Gregorii*, Fra Tomasso da Celano

Preces

Pater Noster

Pater noster, qui es in cælis, sanctificetur nomen tuum. Adveniat regnum tuum, fiat voluntas tua, sicut in cælo et in terrá. Panem nostrum, quotidianum, da nobis hodie. Et dimitte nobis, debita nostra. Sicut et nos dimitimus, debitoribus nostris; et ne nos inducas in tentationem, sed libera nos á malo. Amen.

Ave Maria

Ave Maria, gratiá plená, Dominus tecum. Benedicta tu in mulieribus, et benedictus fructus ventris tui, Jesus. Sancta Maria, mater Dei, ora pro nobis peccatoribus, nunc et in horá mortis nostrae. Amen.

Gloria Patri

Gloria Patri, et Filio, et Spiritui Sancto, sicut erat in principio, et nunc, et semper, et in sæcula sæculorum. Amen.

Common Prayers

Our Father

Our Father, who art in heaven, hallowed by Thy name. Thy kingdom come, Thy will be done, on earth as it is in heaven. Give us this day our daily bread, and forgive us our trespasses, as we forgive those who trespass against us. And lead us not into temptation, but deliver us from evil.

Hail Mary

Hail Mary, full of grace, the Lord is with thee. Blessed art thou amongst women, and blessed is the fruit of thy womb, Jesus. Holy Mary, Mother of God, pray for us sinners, now and at the hour of our death. Amen.

Glory be

Glory be to the Father, and the Son and the Holy Ghost, as it was in the beginning, is now, and ever shall be, world without end. Amen.

Exercitium Sanctæ Crucis
Secundum Sanctum Franciscum

Oratio præparatoria
Suscipe, Sancta Trinitas, hoc servitutis meæ obsequium, quod ad divinæ Maiestatis tuæ gloriam, et recognitionem redemptionis nostræ, pro satisfactione peccatorum meorum ad impetrandam defunctis requiem, vivisque gratiam, omnibus gloriam offero, in unione meritorum Domini nostri Jesu Christi, Beatæ Virginis Mariæ et omnium Sanctorum. Tibi laus, honor, et gloria, o beata Trinitas, in sempiterna sæcula. Amen.

V. Deus in adjutorium meum intende.
R. Domine ad adjuvandum me festina.

Gloria Patri, et Filio, et Spiritui Sancto. Sicut erat in principio, et nunc, et semper, et in sæcula sæculorum. Amen.

Way of the Cross
According to St. Francis

Preparatory prayer
Receive, O holy Trinity, this my dutiful service, which I offer unto You in union with the merits of our Lord Jesus Christ, of the Blessed Virgin, and of all the Saints, to the glory of Your divine majesty, in satisfaction for my sins, in remembrance of our redemption, and to obtain rest for the dead, grace for the living, and for all everlasting glory. To You be praise, and honor, and glory, O blessed Trinity, forever and ever. Amen.

V. O God, come to my assistance.
R. O Lord, make haste to help me.

Glory be to the Father, and to the Son, and to the Holy Ghost. As it was in the beginning, is now, and ever shall be, world without end. Amen.

✠

Prima Statio
Christus ad mortem condemnatur

V. Adoramus te, Domine Jesu Christe, et benedicimus tibi.
R. Quia per sanctam crucem tuam redemisti mundum.

Meditatio:
Innocentissimus Jesus, qui peccatum non fecit nec facere potuit, ad mortem condemnatur, et quidem ad ignominiosam mortem crucis. Ut Pilatus amicus Cæsaris habeatur, tradit Jesum voluntati inimicorum suorum. -- O horrenda injustitia! ut homini placeat, innocentiam damnare et Deum offendere non formidat.

Oratio:
O innocentissime Jesu! ego peccavi: ego mortis æternæ reus sum: ut autem ego vivam, tu sententiam mortis lubens acceptas. Quomodo ergo in posterum vivam, nisi tibi soli? Si hominibus placere cupiam, servus tuus esse non possum: displiceam igitur ipsis et toti mundo, ut tibi soli placere valeam.

Pater Noster.
Jesu Christe crucifixe, miserere mei.

✠

First Station
Jesus is Condemned to Death

V. We adore Thee, O Christ, and we bless Thee.
R. Because by Thy holy Cross Thou hast redeemed the world.

Meditation:
The most innocent Jesus, who did not and could not sin, is condemned to death, and, indeed, to the most ignominious death of the Cross. Pilate delivered Him into the hands of His enemies, that He might remain a friend of Cæsar. O dreadful injustice! He does not fear to condemn innocence and offend God, that he might please men.

Prayer:
O innocent Jesus! I have sinned, and I am guilty of eternal death; but that I may live You gladly receive the sentence of death. How then, shall I live, unless it is for You alone? If I shall desire to please men, I cannot be Your servant: thus may I displease them, and the whole world that I might avail myself to please You alone.

Our Father.
O Jesus Christ crucified, have mercy on me.

✠

Secunda Statio
Jesus suscipit crucem super humeros

V. Adoramus te, Domine Jesu Christe, et benedicimus tibi.
R. Quia per sanctam crucem tuam redemisti mundum.

Meditatio:
Jesus crucem intuens, summo cum desiderio sua brachia sanguine madentia, ad eam extendit illamque tenerrime amplexus, cordintime osculatus, humeris suis vulneribus dilaniatis imponit, et, licet ad mortem usque debilitatus, exultat ut gigas ad currendam viam suam.
Oratio:
Non amicus Christi ero, si inimicus crucis sim! O dulcis, O bona crux! ego te amplector, exosculor et gaudenter suscipio de manu Dei. Absit a me amplius gloriari, nisi in cruce Domini mei, per quam mihi mundus crucifixus sit, et ego mundo: ut totus tuus sim, o Jesu, tuæ Passionis me fac consortem.

Pater Noster.
Jesu Christe crucifixe, miserere mei.

Second Station
Jesus Receives the Cross upon His shoulders

V. We adore Thee, O Christ, and we bless Thee.
R. Because by Thy holy Cross Thou hast redeemed the world.

Meditation:
Jesus Christ beholding the Cross, with the greatest desire, extends His arms soaked in blood to it, very gently embraces it, having tenderly kissed it, places it on His shoulders so torn asunder, and although He is weary unto death, He rejoices as a giant to run the way.

Prayer:
I will not be a friend of Christ if I should be an enemy of the Cross! O sweet, O good Cross! I embrace you, I kiss you, I joyfully accept you from the hand of God. May God forbid me to boast any longer, except in the Cross of my Lord, through which the world has been crucified to me and I to the world, that I may be all Yours. O Jesus, make me a partaker of Your Passion.

Our Father.
O Jesus Christ crucified, have mercy on me.

Tertia Statio
Jesus prima vice cadit sub cruce

V. Adoramus te, Domine Jesu Christe, et benedicimus tibi.
R. Quia per sanctam crucem tuam redemisti mundum.

Meditatio:
Amantissimus Jesus cruce oneratus incendens, ejus pondere depressus graviter in terram prolapsus est. Scilicet peccata nostra pondus illud intolerabile efficiebant, cui alias crux levis et dulcis amore nostri videbatur.

Oratio:
Ah mi Jesu! tu grave jugum peccatorum meorum portasti, et iniquitates meæ sicut onus grave gravatæ sunt super te; cur ergo iugum mandatorum tuorum ferre recusem, ut sic alter alterius onera portemus? Jugum tuum suave est et onus tuum leve: libenter itaque et gaudenter illud suscipiam, et portare contendam, donec vixero. Tu, O Jesu, portantem me gratia tua ita conforta, ne cadam amplius peccando graviter.

Pater Noster.
Jesu Christe crucifixe, miserere mei.

Third Station
Jesus Falls the First Time under the Cross

V. We adore Thee, O Christ, and we bless Thee.
R. Because by Thy holy Cross Thou hast redeemed the world.

Meditation:
The most beloved Jesus, oppressed by the Cross, feverish, bowed low by its weight, violently fell to the ground. Certainly, our sins are the weight which caused that unbearable burden, for whom another cross, on account of the love of us, did not appear light and sweet.

Prayer:
My Jesus! You bore the heavy yoke of my sins, and my iniquities, were loaded down upon You as a heavy burden. How, then, should I refuse to carry the yoke of Your commandments, so each of us might bear the burdens of one another? Your yoke is sweet and Your burden is light: I, therefore, willingly and gladly accept it, and I will strive to carry it, so long as I will have lived. O Jesus, console me while I carry it by Your grace, lest I might violently fall again by sinning.

Our Father.
O Jesus Christ crucified, have mercy on me.

Quarta Statio
Jesus occurrit Matri suæ dolorosissimæ

V. Adoramus te, Domine Jesu Christe, et benedicimus tibi.
R. Quia per sanctam crucem tuam redemisti mundum.

Meditatio:
Quam dolorosus erat aspectus afflictissimæ Matris Mariæ, dilectissimum Filium suum gravi cruce onustum, totum vulneribus et sanguine scatentem, ab infami fæce carnificum tanta rabie impulsum conspicientis! Quam ineffabiles dolores sensit illud tenerrimum cor maternum! O quam desiderabat pro Jesu, vel saltem cum Jesu mori!

Oratio:
O Jesu! O Maria! ego sum causa dolorum cordium vestrorum, summe invicem amantium et ad extremum usque desolatorum. Ah utinam et cor meum de vestro dolore participet! -- Eia, Mater, fons amoris, me sentire vim doloris fac, ut tecum lugeam. Fac, ut ardeat cor meum in amando Christum Deum, ut sibi complaceam. Hoc demum a te humiliter efflagito, ut et mihi in amarissimæ huius Passionis vestræ memoria mortis semitam intranti, materna pietate occurrere et cum Filio tuo dulcissimo succurrere digneris.

Pater Noster.
Jesu Christe crucifixe, miserere mei.

✠

Fourth Station
Jesus Meets His Most Sorrowful Mother

V. We adore Thee, O Christ, and we bless Thee.
R. Because by Thy holy Cross Thou hast redeemed the world.

Meditation:
How sorrowful was the most afflicted Mother Mary's glance, of seeing her beloved Son laden with the burden of the Cross, His whole body gushing with wounds and blood, being struck by disreputable dregs of executioners with such madness! How that most tender maternal heart sensed unspeakable pains! How it longed for Jesus, or at least to die with Him!
Prayer:
O Jesus! O Mary! I am the cause of the pains of Your loving hearts, in turn from the very highest point to the limit of desolation. O, that my heart also would share in Your sufferings! Mother, font of love, make me sense the force of this pain, that I might weep with you. See to it, that my heart should burn in the love of the Christ-God, so that I might embrace Him. I ask at least this, humbly from you, that you would vouchsafe by your maternal piety, that I run, entering into the way of death by the memory of this your most bitter passion, and to aid me with your most sweet Son.
Our Father.
O Jesus Christ crucified, have mercy on me.

Quinta Statio
Jesus a Simone Cyreneo in bajulatione crucis adiuvatur

V. Adoramus te, Domine Jesu Christe, et benedicimus tibi.
R. Quia per sanctam crucem tuam redemisti mundum.

Meditatio:
Simon Cyrenæus angariatur ad tollendam crucem post Jesum, propter scelera nostra attritum ac debilitatum, quem, licet renitentem, Jesus pro comite acceptat. O quam gratus hic in Passione socius foret, si non coacte, sed sponte venisset. Sed etiam te, o anima mea, libenter acceptaret, si velles. Vocat te, invitat te: Tolle crucem tuam et sequere me, Tu vero resistis, et pro pudore! non nisi coacte crucem suscipis.

Oratio:
O Jesu! quam vere dixisti: "Qui non accipit crucem suam et sequitur me, non est me dignus" -- En! ut dignus te efficiar, ultro me comitem tibi in via crucis iungo: feram lubens tribulationem et crucem, si non tuam gravissimam, saltem illam meam, quamcumque demum humeris imponere meis tibi placuerit; hanc, sequendo te, portabo patiens usque ad finem vitæ meæ.

Pater Noster.
Jesu Christe crucifixe, miserere mei.

✠

Fifth Station
Simon of Cyrene Helps Jesus to Carry the Cross

V. We adore Thee, O Christ, and we bless Thee.
R. Because by Thy holy Cross Thou hast redeemed the world.
Meditation:
Simon of Cyrene is constrained to carry the cross behind Jesus, wasted and crippled on account of our sins. Jesus receives him for a companion, although he is reluctant. O, how pleasing this companion would have been in the Passion, if he would have come not by coercion, but from His own will. Yet, even you, O my soul, He shall gladly accept, if you wish. He calls you, He invites you: 'Take your cross and follow Me,' but you resist, and what shame! You do not receive it except by coercion!
Prayer:
O Jesus! How truly You said: "Whosoever does not take up his cross and follow Me is not worthy of Me." Lo! That I should become worthy of You, I join myself to You as a companion on the way of the cross: I shall gladly carry Your distress and the cross, if not Your heaviest, then at least let that one be mine, whichever at the last You will have been pleased to place upon my shoulders: I shall carry this by following You, suffering even to the end of my life.
Our Father.
O Jesus Christ crucified, have mercy on me.

Sexta Statio
Veronica Christo sudarium præsentat

V. Adoramus te, Domine Jesu Christe, et benedicimus tibi.
R. Quia per sanctam crucem tuam redemisti mundum.

Meditatio:
Veronica ex compassione et devotione velum capitis sui Jesu porrexit ad abstergendam faciem suam, sanguine et sputis defœdatam. Ille autem vultus sui effigiem eidem impressam restituit. O exiguum obsequium præstas tu, o anima mea, Salvatori tuo pro tot immensis beneficiis? recogita, dole et emendationem propone.

Oratio:
O Jesu! quid retribuam tibi pro omnibus, quæ retribuisti mihi? totum me consecro servitio tuo: totum cor meum tibi offero: pone te ut signaculum super illud, et imprime imaginem tuam, ut jugiter memoria memor sim tui, nec tu operis tui obliviscaris in finem.

Pater Noster.
Jesu Christe crucifixe, miserere mei.

✠

Sixth Station
Veronica presents the veil to Christ

V. We adore Thee, O Christ, and we bless Thee.
R. Because by Thy holy Cross Thou hast redeemed the world.
Meditation:
Veronica, by her devotion and compassion, stretches out the veil of her own head to Jesus to wipe His face, defiled by blood and spit. Yet He restored the image of His countenance imprinted upon it; O what scanty attendance you offer to your Saviour, my soul, for so many immense benefits! Reflect with pain, and offer amendment.
Prayer:
O Jesus! What shall I render unto You, for all the things that You have rendered unto me? I consecrate myself entirely to Your service. I offer You my whole heart: place Yourself as a seal over it, and impress Your image, that I might continuously be mindful of You, that You should not forget Your work in the end.

Our Father.
O Jesus Christ crucified, have mercy on me.

✠

Septima Statio
Secundus lapsus Jesu ad portam

V. Adoramus te, Domine Jesu Christe, et benedicimus tibi.
R. Quia per sanctam crucem tuam redemisti mundum.

Meditatio:
Dolorosissimus Jesus iterum sub crucis pondere jacet, sacratissima sua facie in terram prostratus, nec a diabolica crudelitate carnificum momentum quietis ipsi datur, funibus et fustibus ad progrediendum compellitur. Hunc lapsum causarunt peccata nostra reiterata, et ego amplius peccare delecter?

Oratio:
O Jesu! miserere mei, porrige dexteram tuam, sustenta me, ne amplius in peccata priora relabar. Ergone peccatum hoc N. N. sciens volens repetam? absit a me. Dixi, nunc cœpi; ab hoc momento serio conclusum sit, millies mori, quam peccare. Tu, mi Jesu, conforta me per gratiam tuam, sine qua nihil possum.

Pater Noster.
Jesu Christe crucifixe, miserere mei.

✠

Seventh Station
The Second fall of Jesus at the gate

V. We adore Thee, O Christ, and we bless Thee.
R. Because by Thy holy Cross Thou hast redeemed the world.

Meditation:
The most suffering Jesus, falls again under the weight of His Cross, having struck the ground with His most sacred face; nor is He given a moment of rest by the diabolic cruelty of His executioners. He is forced, by ropes and clubs to continue. Our repeated sins have caused this fall, and yet, am I pleased to sin further?

Prayer:
O Jesus! Have mercy on me! Extend to me Your right hand and support me, lest I should fall again into my old sins. Shall I, therefore, knowing this sin (N.) willingly repeat it? I have said it, now I begin: from this very moment, let it be decided, to die a thousand times rather than sin. You, O Jesus, comfort me through Your grace, without which I cannot continue.

Our Father.
O Jesus Christ crucified, have mercy on me.

✠

Octava Statio
Jesus filias Jerusalem flentes alloquitur

V. Adoramus te, Domine Jesu Christe, et benedicimus tibi.
R. Quia per sanctam crucem tuam redemisti mundum.

Meditatio:
Devotæ hæ mulieres plorant dolentes super Salvatorem, ipse autem ad eas conversus ait: "Nolite flere super me innocentem, sed super vos ipsas flete et super filios vestros", super peccata vestra flete utpote causam omnium horum dolorum. Ergo et tu plora, anima mea! nihil gratius est Christo tibique nihil utilius, quam lacrimæ, ex dolore de peccatis profusæ.
Oratio:
O Jesu! quis dabit capiti meo aquam et oculis meis fontem lacrimarum, ut die ac nocte defleam peccata mea? Per amaras, sanguineas lacrimas tuas te oro, concede mihi donum lacrimarum: contere cor meum, ut ex oculis et corde copiosæ lacrimæ profluant et peccata mea vera contritione exstinguant.

Pater Noster.
Jesu Christe crucifixe, miserere mei.

✠

Eighth Station
Jesus addresses the weeping daughters of Jerusalem

V. We adore Thee, O Christ, and we bless Thee.
R. Because by Thy holy Cross Thou hast redeemed the world.

Meditation:
These devoted women, are grieving over the Saviour. He, however, turns to them, saying: "Weep not for Me Who am innocent, but weep for yourselves and for your children." Weep over your sins, in as much as they are the cause of all these sufferings. Therefore, you also must weep, my soul! Nothing is more agreeable to Christ and nothing more useful to you, than tears, shed from the pain with regard to sins.

Prayer:
O Jesus! Who will give water to my head and a fountain of tears to my eyes, that day and night I may weep for my sins? I ask You, grant through Your sad and bloody tears that I might receive the gift of tears; crush my heart, that from my eyes and heart bountiful tears might flow, and might extinguish my sins with true contrition.

Our Father.
O Jesus Christ crucified, have mercy on me.

Nona Statio
Jesus ad ascensum montis Calvariæ tertio cadit

V. Adoramus te, Domine Jesu Christe, et benedicimus tibi.
R. Quia per sanctam crucem tuam redemisti mundum.

Meditatio:
Jesus despectus et novissimus virorum, vir dolorum, et sciens infirmitatem, quam pro nobis assumpsit et pertulit, pedem montis Calvariæ attingens, jam tertio gravissime prolapsus est, dolorosissime allisus in saxum ibidem in via positum. O quam immane pondus est peccatum! Jesum toties in terram depressit, et me jam dudum in abyssum inferni detrusisset, nisi pretiosa merita sanctissimæ Passionis ejus me præservassent.
Oratio:
O clementissime Jesu! infinitas tibi gratias ago, quod me toties peccantem peccatis meis nec immori, nec, prout centies merebar, in profundum inferni præcipitari permiseris. Accende in me novum fervorem, fove hunc jugiter meque in tua conserva gratia, ne unquam amplius ea excidam, aut cadam retro, sed in bono confirmatus de corpore mortis hujus transeam ad libertatem filiorum Dei perfectam.

Pater Noster.
Jesu Christe crucifixe, miserere mei.

✠

Ninth Station
Jesus falls the third time on the ascent to Calvary

V. We adore Thee, O Christ, and we bless Thee.
R. Because by Thy holy Cross Thou hast redeemed the world.
Meditation:
Jesus, despised and utmost of men, a man of sorrows, knowing weakness, which He took up and bore for us, reaching the foot of mount of Calvary, now falls violently for the third time, crushed most painfully onto a rock placed in that very spot. O, how savage is the weight of sin! As many times as it pushed Jesus down to the ground, already long ago it would have thrust me into the abyss of hell, except that the precious merits of His most holy passion preserved me.
Prayer:
Most merciful Jesus! I thank You for the infinite occasions, when I was sinning, that You did not permit me to die for my sins, nor, in as much as I deserved it a hundred times, to fall headlong into the depths of hell. Enkindle in me a new fervor, foster this continually in me and preserve me in Your grace, lest I should ever again cut them off, or fall back into sin, rather being confirmed in good, may I cross from the body of this death to the perfect freedom of the sons of God.
Our Father.
O Jesus Christ crucified, have mercy on me.

✠

Decima Statio
Jesus vestibus nudatur et felle potatur

V. Adoramus te, Domine Jesu Christe, et benedicimus tibi.
R. Quia per sanctam crucem tuam redemisti mundum.

Meditatio:
Detrahuntur, vel potius violenta rabie diripiuntur Jesu meo vestes suæ. Ah! quanto cum dolore, dum etiam cutis una cum iisdem sanguine conglutinata dolorosissime avellitur. Exuitur vestibus, ut nudus moriatur. O quam bene, quam feliciter morerer, si veterem hominem cum actibus suis exutus decederem!

Oratio:
Fiat, mi Jesu, fiat, ut exuam veterem hominem, et induam novum secundum cor et voluntatem tuam creatum. Et licet sensualitati meæ amarum accidat, non tamen parcam cuti meæ. Omnibus mundanis vanitatibus nudatus mori cupio, ut tecum vivam in æternum.

Pater Noster.
Jesu Christe crucifixe, miserere mei.

✠

Tenth Station
Jesus is Stripped of His Garments and offered gall

V. We adore Thee, O Christ, and we bless Thee.
R. Because by Thy holy Cross Thou hast redeemed the world.

Meditation:
Your garments are stripped off, O my Jesus, or rather with insane violence ripped off. O! With what pain is it most excruciatingly taken away, even while the skin cleaved to the same with blood. Stripped from His garments, that He should die naked. O, how well, how happily shall I die, if being stripped I should lay aside the old man with his acts!

Prayer:
Let it be done, O my Jesus, let it be done, that I should strip off the old man, and shall put on the new, created according to Your heart and will. And although it should happen to be bitter to my sensuality, nevertheless, I shall not spare my flesh. I desire to die naked to all mundane vanities, that I might live with You in eternity.

Our Father.
O Jesus Christ crucified, have mercy on me.

Undecima Statio
Jesu cruci affigitur

V. Adoramus te, Domine Jesu Christe, et benedicimus tibi.
R. Quia per sanctam crucem tuam redemisti mundum.

Meditatio:
Jesus vestibus spoliatus in cruce crudeliter extenditur et pedibus manibusque horrendis clavis affigitur. O cruciatus! o dolor! et ipse silet, quia amore mei patitur. O anima mea! quomodo tu te geris in afflictionibus tuis? quam impatienter, quam querulose suffers eas!

Oratio:
O patientissime Jesu, Agne mansuetissime! detestor et abominor omnem impatientiam meam. Eia, Domine, crucifige carnem meam cum concupiscentiis et vitiis suis; hic ure, hic seca, ut in æternum parcas. Totum me projicio in manus tuas, tua sancta voluntas in omnibus fiat. Solam gratiam tuam mihi dona, et sufficit mihi.

Pater Noster.
Jesu Christe crucifixe, miserere mei.

Eleventh Station
Jesus is Nailed to the Cross

V. We adore Thee, O Christ, and we bless Thee.
R. Because by Thy holy Cross Thou hast redeemed the world.

Meditation:
Jesus, after being despoiled of His clothes, is cruelly stretched upon the Cross, and He is pierced in His hands and His feet by dreadful nails! O what torture! O what pain! And He is silent, because He suffers for the love of me, — O my soul! How can you stand yourself in your afflictions? How impatiently, how querulous you suffer these things!

Prayer:
O most patient Jesus, most gentle Lamb! I curse and abhor all my impatience. O Lord, crucify my flesh together with its concupiscence and vices. Burn here, cut here, that You might spare in eternity. I cast myself entirely into Your hands, let Your holy will be done in all things. Give me Your grace alone, and it will be enough.

Our Father.
O Jesus Christ crucified, have mercy on me.

Duodecima Statio
Jesus in cruce levatur et moritur

V. Adoramus te, Domine Jesu Christe, et benedicimus tibi.
R. Quia per sanctam crucem tuam redemisti mundum.

Meditatio:
Aspice Jesum in cruce pendentem, nudum et vulneribus abundantem, inspice plagas, quas amore tui recepit. Tota eius figura est typus amoris: caput inclinatum ad osculandum te, brachia extensa ad amplectendum te; quot vulnera, tot pignora amoris Jesu tui amantissimi. O quantus est hic amor! Jesus moritur, ut peccator vivat et ab æterna morte liberetur; sed eheu! hic amor, tantus cum sit, quam male rependitur!

Oratio:
Amantissime Jesu! quis dabit mihi, ut amore tui moriar; fac me saltem mundi vanitatibus amore tui totaliter mori. O quam sordet mihi mundus, si te in cruce pendentem aspicio! Suscipe me, O Jesu, in transfixum Cor tuum. Totus sum tuus, nec vivere volo nec mori, nisi tibi.

Pater Noster.
Jesu Christe crucifixe, miserere mei.

✠

Twelfth Station
Jesus is lifted up and dies on the Cross

V. We adore Thee, O Christ, and we bless Thee.
R. Because by Thy holy Cross Thou hast redeemed the world.

Meditation:
Behold Jesus hanging on the cross, naked and overflowing with wounds, inspect the blow, which He received for love of you. His whole form is a type of love; His head is lowered to kiss you, His arms are outstretched to embrace you; as many as there are wounds, there are pledges of the love of your most beloved Jesus. O how great is this love! Jesus is dead, that a sinner might live and be freed from eternal death; but alas! This love, although it is so great, is so badly repaid!

Prayer:
O most beloved Jesus! Who will grant me that I might die for You; make me At least provide that I die completely to the vanities of the world for love of You. O, how the world is vile to me, if I look upon You hanging on the cross! Receive me, O Jesus, fastened onto Your Heart. All I am is Yours, I wish neither to live nor die, unless it is for You.

Our Father.
Jesus Christ crucified, have mercy on me.

Tredecima Statio
Jesus de cruce deponitur

V. Adoramus te, Domine Jesu Christe, et benedicimus tibi.
R. Quia per sanctam crucem tuam redemisti mundum.

Meditatio:
Noluit Jesus de cruce vivus descendere, sed usque ad mortem in ea hærere. Cum autem mortuus deponeretur, voluit, uti vivus, sic et mortuus, in gremio virginali SS. Matris suæ cubare. Esto et tu constans in bonis propositis, nec de cruce tua descendas: qui enim perseveraverit usque ad finem, hic salvus erit. Cogita simul, quanta puritate oporteat cor illud nitere, in quod corpus Jesu in SS. Sacramento recipitur.

Oratio:
O Jesu! deprecor te, ne permittas me de cruce tua avelli; in ea enim vivere cupio et mori. Crea in me, Deus, cor mundum, ut per S. Communionem sacratissimum Corpus tuum digne recipiam et in te maneam, nec unquam a te valeam separari.

Pater Noster.
Jesu Christe crucifixe, miserere mei.

✠

Thirteenth Station
Jesus is Taken Down From the Cross

V. We adore Thee, O Christ, and we bless Thee.
R. Because by Thy holy Cross Thou hast redeemed the world.
Meditation:
Jesus refused to come down from the Cross alive, rather to cling to it even unto death. And when He was taken down from it, He wished, even in death, as He had in life, to rest in the virginal lap of His most holy Mother. Be steadfast in your good resolutions lest you might descend from the cross; he who will have persevered to the end will be saved. Ponder likewise, in what purity that heart ought to shine, in which the body of Jesus is received in the most blessed Sacrament.
Prayer:
O Jesus! I beg You, lest You permit me to be torn away from Your cross. Indeed, I desire to live and die on it. Create in me, O God, a clean heart, that I might worthily receive Your most Holy body in Holy Communion, and remain in You, and that I might avail myself to never be separated from You.

Our Father.
O Jesus Christ crucified, have mercy on me.

Quartadecima Statio
Sepultura Christi

V. Adoramus te, Domine Jesu Christe, et benedicimus tibi.
R. Quia per sanctam crucem tuam redemisti mundum.

Meditatio:
Corpus Christi sepultum est in alieno monumento. Qui in cruce non habuit, ubi SS. Caput suum reclinaret, nec proprium sepulchrum invenit in mundo quia nempe non erat de hoc mundo. Tu qui tantum dependes ab hoc, numquid es de illo? Sed fuge, contemne eum, ne cum ipso pereas.

Oratio:
O Jesu, tu me elegisti de hoc mundo, quid mihi ergo cum illo? Tu me creasti ad cælum, quid jam a te mihi volo super terram, in qua proh dolor! multum incola fuit anima mea? Apage, o munde, cum vanitatibus tuis; in via crucis, quam Salvator meus suis sacris signavit vestigiis, incedam impiger et tendam ad patriam cælestem, ubi habitatio et requies mea sit in æternum.

Pater Noster.
Jesu Christe crucifixe, miserere mei.

Fourteenth Station
The burial of Christ

V. We adore Thee, O Christ, and we bless Thee.
R. Because by Thy holy Cross Thou hast redeemed the world.

Meditation:
The body of Christ has been buried in someone else's tomb. He who did not have on the cross, a place to rest His most holy head, neither found His own tomb in the world, rightly, because He was not of the world. You, who depend upon this world, can it be that you are of it? Rather flee, condemn it, lest you also perish with it.

Prayer:
O Jesus! You have chosen me from this world; what, then, is there for me in it? You created me for heaven; what, then, do I want for myself from You in a world in which I suffer? Away with you, O world, with your vanities! I shall eagerly march on the way of the Cross which my Saviour signed with His sacred footprints, and I shall make for that heavenly homeland, where there is dwelling and rest in eternity.

Our Father.
O Jesus Christ crucified, have mercy on me.

Rosarium Seraphicum

Frequens devotio quæ inter membra tertiæ ordinis S. Francisci invenitur est Rosarium Seraphicum, sive Corona, et enim devotio laudabilis universi Ecclesiæ sit.

In sequenti modo orari possit:
In nomine Patris, et Filii, et Spiritus Sancti.
R. Amen.
V. Deus in Adjutorium meum intend.
R. Domine, ad adjuvandum me festina.
Gloria Patri, etc.

Prima Exaltatio Mariæ: de Annuntione et Maternitate sua.
Pater Noster; Ave Maria, decies; Gloria Patri.

Secunda Exaltatio Mariæ: de Visitatione sua ad S. Elizabetham.
Pater Noster; Ave Maria, decies; Gloria Patri.

Tertia Exultatio: de Nativitate Jesu.
Pater Noster; Ave Maria, decies; Gloria Patri.

Quarta exultatio: de Adoratione Magorum.
Pater Noster; Ave Maria, decies; Gloria Patri.

Quinta exultatio: de Inventione Jesu in Templo.
Pater Noster; Ave Maria, decies; Gloria Patri.

Sexta exultatio: de Resurrectione gloriosa Divini Filii sui.
Pater Noster; Ave Maria, decies; Gloria Patri.

Seraphic Rosary

A Frequent devotion found amongst the members of the third order of St. Francis is the Seraphic Rosary, also called the Corona. It is indeed, a praiseworthy devotion for the whole Church and may be prayed thus:

In the name of the Father, and of the Son, and of the Holy Ghost.
R. Amen
V. O God, come to my assistance.
R. O Lord make haste to help me.
Glory be, etc.

The First joy of Mary at her Annunciation and Divine Maternity.
One *Our Father,* Ten *Hail Marys, Glory be.*

The Second joy of Mary at her Visit to St. Elizabeth
One *Our Father,* Ten *Hail Marys, Glory be.*

The Third joy of Mary, at the birth of Jesus.
One *Our Father,* Ten *Hail Marys, Glory be.*

The Fourth joy of Mary, on the Adoration of the Magi.
One *Our Father,* Ten *Hail Marys, Glory be.*

The Fifth joy of Mary, on the finding of Jesus in the Temple.
One *Our Father,* Ten *Hail Marys, Glory be.*

The Sixth joy of Mary, at the Glorious Resurrection of her Divine Son.
One *Our Father,* Ten *Hail Marys, Glory be.*

Septima Exultatio: de Assumptione sua in cælum, corpore et anima.
Pater Noster; Ave Maria, decies; Gloria Patri.

    Bis amplius *Ave Maria* dicitur, deinde semel *Pater* et *Ave Maria* pro Summo Pontifice. Rosarium ita concluditur:

V. In Conceptione tua, Virgo, immaculata fuisti.
R. Ora pro nobis Patrem, cujus Filium peperisti.

Oremus.
    Deus, qui per Immaculatam Virginis Conceptionem, dignum Filio tuo habitaculum præparasti, quæsumus, ut qui ex morte ejusdem Filii sui prævisa eam ab omni labe præservasti, nos quoque mundos, ejus intercessione ad te pervenire concedas. Per eundum Christum Dominum nostrum. Amen.

Coronatio Beatae Virginis
- Rubens

The seventh joy of Mary, on her Assumption into heaven in body and in soul.
One *Our Father,* Ten *Hail Marys, Glory be.*

Two more Hail Marys are said, then an Our Father and a Hail Mary for the Sovereign Pontiff. Then it is concluded with the following prayers:

V. In thy Conception, O Virgin Mary, thou were immaculate.
R. Pray for us to the Father, whose Son thou brought forth.

Let us pray.
    O God, who prepared for thy Son a worthy habitation, by the Immaculate Conception of the Blessed Virgin Mary, we beseech Thee that, as Thou, who did preserve her from every stain of sin, through the merits of the preordained death of the same Son, would grant that we also, having been cleansed by her intercession, might come to Thee. Through the Same Christ our Lord. Amen.

Coronation of the
Blessed Virgin
-Rubens

OTHER FRANCISCAN BOOKS AVAILABLE FROM
MEDIATRIX PRESS

The Life of St. Francis of Assisi

Brothre Deo Gratias - The life of St. Felix of Cantalice

St. John Capistran, a Reformer in Battle

The Autobiography of St. Charles of Sezze

Walled in Light: The life of St. Collette

The Seraphic Order: A Traditional Franciscan Book of Saints

www.ingramcontent.com/pod-product-compliance
Lightning Source LLC
Chambersburg PA
CBHW010004110526
44587CB00024BA/4017